The First

by B. Grissom

dedicated to bittersweet first love

contents

Love..7

Lust..45

Loss...75

Love

my secret hobby

These words
are everything
I want you to know.
All that lives below,
some of which, frankly,
I'm scared to show.
They're everything I don't say
for it'd sound too cheesy and cliché.
Together they create
a living diary
of my devoted days,
destined to feel your gaze.
Some you'll recognize,
and others, I hope,
take your breath away.
My heart was bled
on every page,
please remember that
as your hands upon them you lay.

aged to perfection

I love the way love
never grows old
and the way the prettiest things
only get prettier with age.
I love how your warmth
drives away
the bitterest of colds
and how, just like a flower,
I'm free to bloom
on my pick of the days.
I love the me I am with you
and how, out of everyone,
you picked me too.

sprouting so many words

I wonder if she'd ever guess
this book is about her,
from beginning to end
she's in every last word.
A lovelorn mind kept up
tossing and turning at night
until the words are coughed up
peace is out of sight.
Driven to inspiration or madness,
call it what you will,
with poems about her, for her,
these pages I will continue to fill.

self-sacrificed for her

I love with every inch of my being
  simply because
    I know no other way.
I drain myself
to fill you up
until your bedrock
    the very core of who you are
is as saturated
    as the day after
        God's greatest storm.
Alas, there is no suffering sweeter
    than to see you rise up
      as I am sinking
        worn and depleted.

give me more of her

There's a girl I'd like to know.
She has your laugh
and she wears your clothes.
She's the you
    you've hidden underneath
but to me she subtlety speaks.
If I'm lucky,
    every now and then,
I can catch a peek.
Just the tiniest glimpse
    of her ascent.
A shimmer in your eye
gives her away, every time.

a fallen plea

Breathe back into me
    the life
I thought was gone
    the passion
I thought had died
    the joy
I could no longer
  bring to mind

reincarnated

It takes all of
a fraction of a second
to surrender myself unto you.
Caving in
with the glance of an eye
or the brush of lips.
And I fear it'll take
more than a few lifetimes
to ever change my ways.

in living beats

What would I say
if I had just fifty words
to open your ears
to my heart's chords?
 To a symphony
 no one hears?
Could it even be done?

Every composing cell
Is drenched
With love they swell
My bones
Whistle and hum
Until to you
They can run
Vibrations ripple
Outward from within
Pulsating arteries
Hold the beat
Invigorating life
Beneath the skin
In step
My body moves
Flowing along
In sync
With the groove
Of loving you

an admirer's desire

I long to be...

the hand that holds yours
the mind of which you never bore
the name tattooed on your heart
the one you hate to part
the shoulder that catches your tears
the smile that eases your fears
the embrace you crave
the love behind your rave

...simply yours

to be the one

Won't you lay down?
The space is free
next to me.
From my arms to my feet
let my body mold
to the shape of your sleep.
Put your mind to rest
and lay down your head
upon my chest.

how can you love incompletely

I do not know how
to love in *parts* and *pieces*
You have my whole heart

why can't you see

I love you
and I'm trying
to make you see
I know no other
way to be.
Existing in a world
where everything is better
when you're with me.
The only constant
of my dreams;
with no one else
a future can I conceive.
From your side
I would never leave,
for in love with you,
   please believe,
is all I'll ever be.

I'll break it down

loves a lie
but with you
it was worth
believin'

Oh, what am I sayin'
ain't no one
I'm deceivin'

I love you still
it's my heart
you've been thievin'

The chemistry
between us
it's all anyones
perceivin'

grace and beauty

I didn't know I was staring,
frozen in a moment
like a pendulum in mid-swing
Stuck in those still seconds
with music
filling up the room
and you
dancing all around without a clue
that I'd walked in
and caught you
Into something secret
and beautiful
I stumbled

Frozen I stood
soaking it all in
before my cover crumbled
and staring I couldn't help
for in those still seconds
once again, I fell

that's how I see you

I see you
peeking through
the façade you have sewn
I see you
and the truths you try not to show
your shadowed soul
and desires pushed down low
are not hidden from me
      I see you

I see you
in all the unfiltered beauty
one can behold
an unpolished rawness
that calls out to me
and to you, I promise,
your secrets I will keep
because I see you
and I know you see me

it keeps me up at night

you are the storm
   abruptly yanking me
from my peaceful sleep
the flashing of your
electrostatically charged lights
   overwhelms
my weary bloodshot eyes

you are the otherworldly rumble
a delightful deitious delusion
spurring the misfires
of my paralyzed pulse

you pull me back to life
and my only regret
is that I slept through
any of it at all

it keeps me waiting

Here I am
patiently awaiting
you, my thief,
to come
   take me away
to steal
this heart of mine
it longs to be yours
to know
the feel of floating
side by side
it begs
to be taken
and cherished
like nothing else
has been cherished
   take from me
the night
and bathe me
in your light
watch as I blossom
   steal from me
this idea
that something
hardened
can never be
softened
   steal and take
   from me
every hesitation
that I alone
cannot shake

a burrowing love

But no matter what I do
I can't get you off my mind.
All day and through the night
drifting through this life
with your memory on constant replay.

Every song I sing
and every rhyme I write
there you are
in every line.
I can search all my life
and never find another you
that stalks me
quite the same way.

twisted

like a vine
on a tree
you grow on me
everyday
wrapping
and weaving
muscle and bone
inbetween
until indistinguishable
are the two leaves
you are imbedded
in me
an impression
I cannot cleave

stirring

love stirred
and boundaries
blurred
perspective tangled
and meanings
mangled
swirling around
nowhere
bound

this is different

toss aside any
preconceived notions you hold
for there is no reference
to this love we know

all that you are

She talked of repayment
    for my love
but what she failed to understand
    was that
I only wanted her
    broken or whole
        just as she was

naturally

    I want to melt away
        into and with you
      like the hypnotic river water
roaring over rocks
    and trickling through trees
        wholly unstoppable
           and completely free

better than oxygen

your words
are my air
I breathe them in
and without knowing it
they sustain me
there is nothing
special about them
except that
they are yours
without them
I deflate
but with them
I fly to heights
I never even
dreamed to see

a good kind of scared

I've always had a fear of heights
    but I've also always
  craved the thrill of falling.
Roller coasters, water slides
    or high dives
   I'll take it all
  to let, just for a split second,
  chaos take over my insides.
I never would have guessed
   in your eyes, your smile, your touch
   or simply the way you undress
that my thrill could be found.
You're my forever ride
    an exhilarating love
  that can't be held down.

Further and further I climb
    for just a single kiss
leaving all fear choking behind.
    Know, I risk it all
      for you,
          the only one I'll ever fall

it all comes together

On the surface it may seem
that these words follow
no poetic scheme
    Sometimes they lack
rhythm or rhyme
but rest assured
they are keeping time
    The only beat they know–
the erratic ticking
of my heart's metronome
    If you hear them in tune
know it's because no longer
do our hearts beat as two

I hope it never leaves

The ghost of your lips haunts mine.
All I have to do is sit back,
    float away
  just by closing my eyes
to a place where there is
    neither you
      nor I
but rather a swirling kaleidoscope
    of us.
Are you also haunted by my touch?
If your eyes shut with mine
would you too float as such
    meeting me
  in the place
      where there is
          only us?

I will

These eyes
will always shine for you.
These hands
will always hold you.
This soul
will always crave you.
This heart
will never hurt you.
This love
will always burn for you.
This me
will always want for you.

weather

when the flares of your
uncertainty and self-doubt
lash out and scorch
all of your surrounds
I will remain
steadfast as ever
so loyally bound
immovable in my resolve
to show you
not just how
to weather the storms
but how to be rid of them
once and for all

my predicament

I can live without you
I'd just rather not.
In your net
I am forever caught.

I can love another besides you,
it just wouldn't be the same.
My lips are frozen
in the shape of your name.

my addiction problems

It simply does not do
not having you near.

If I gave into the ache
it would surely break me.

How unimaginable though
the probability
of pausing a heart
that beats so strong for you.

How unlikely it is
that this undeniable craving
will ever subdue.

the honest promises

I will kiss
and kiss
and kiss
until you no longer miss

I will whisper
and soothe
and caress
until you no longer stress

I will stand
and weather
and shout
until you no longer doubt

I will love
and love
and love
until this world
we're no longer a part of

lost in your eyes

The shimmer of the city lights
against the fading dusk
of an Oklahoma sky
strikes a nerve
     one
that is usually reserved
for the blue of your eyes
when they peer through mine
polka-dotting my soul
with a million little goosebumps
A feeling
I love that I cannot control

just jump

Follow the light of the stars
and break the streak of nights
of two hearts so far.

Come, escape with me
where the flickering flames
melt away the daily grime
and no claim can stress lay
to what is our time.

Let's make the escape,
leave this crazy ole world
fading, farther and farther behind.
Find my hand, take ahold
and enter a realm of only two-fold.

I'll be here

I (the imperfect being that is I)
    do not know how to fix you
    (the mysterious being that is you);
    your damaged and missing pieces
    are unknown to me.
    All I can ever know
    is the puzzle left behind.
But I
    (the loyal lover I)
    can promise you
    (the perfect for me you)
    that I will fashion new pieces
    to fill every gap
    with this crafty heart of mine.

waiting in winter

Behind these imperfect words
and casual actions,
beyond all the
missed connections
and miscommunications,
there lives a love,
hibernating
and anticipating
a spring-time
vivificating.
Though soundly it sleeps,
a home forever found
in its cardiac niche,
you'd be surprised
how little it takes
to turn dormant awake.

Lust

just a few strands

If I promise to
grasp it just right
intertwined betwixt my fingers,
will you promise to
always let it flow
tickling the bones lying within?

when you're not here

Sometimes it just has to be said
minutes, seconds,
even hours on end
I can't seem to get you
out of my head.
It would be crazy
to try to pretend
you aren't the one
who makes these legs
want to spread.

when you're near

The soft closing
  of lids over
     eyes
the gentle reaching
       of a hand
around my side
    skin on skin
        chest on chest
a tingle
runs
down
my
spine
     the effortless joining
       of your energy
         with mine

distance doesn't matter

Can you feel the waves too?...
Rhythm flowing
in through me
but out through you.

I know you're tempted

What I wouldn't give
    to feel your back
    succumbing to a yearn
  to let my hands
    expertly track
around your curves
navigating
  the tremors
    of my touch
 jolting
    through your flesh
Take as little or as much
  just let our beings intermesh
slowly free me
  from buttons that bind
  and delicately
I'll kiss your neck
  sensuality redefined
  in the essence
  of your skin
    under mine
Give in... lose control
and I'll take you where
  you've never been
    ... if I can be so bold

it's all your fault

If I'm sweet
it's because nothing
turns me on
like
when our skin meets.

There is no room
for intimidation
when you're the reason
for this bold infatuation.

As I watch

The sway of your hips
I can't stop imagining
how from them clothes slip

I'll always remember

memories
glisten in the light
as from my eaves
snow takes flight
the second act
of the magic that
happened last night
a mental playback
tenaciously unceasing
even as the wonderland
around me
is swiftly fleeing

rolling in sin

  I'm the wandering hand
and the shivers
cascading down your spine.
  I'm the little voice
beckoning you
to enter the forbidden garden
and see what you might find.
Take a bite and
let the nectar drip
from your lips.
Embrace the metamorphosis
 ...and tell me,
how long have you dreamt of this?
Surrender.
Indulge.
Act out all you've held in.
  I am the living embodiment
of your temptations.
Forget venial and mortal,
  I am your greatest sin.

worn out

like a ghost
warmth clings to my skin
as behind a cloud
the sun slips
still no match
for the heat left
by trails of fingertips

imagination ain't good enough

There's a dirty side to you
that I only got to sample

just a little taste,

and I tell you
it's such a shame
you never got to explore
my similarly dirty ways

the absence

let it slip, just so
let it slide
       and let it
              fall
these floors were made
for catching
unwanted clothes
come closer
  closer still
these empty arms
are long overdue
their fill

the balance

like a dance
we never had to rehearse
the music moved within us
   so graceful
you always knew
when to spin
   so purposeful
I always knew
when to dip
happily trading
the lead
spinning around
as one
in a truly rare
synchronicity

filled with burning questions

Is there any chance
I could seduce you tonight?
If I stared long enough
would you get lost
in these icy blue eyes?

Tell me,
if I promise to be gentle
and take my time
could my fingertips trace
flesh covered outlines
until every inch of velvet
has been taken in?

And if my hand
should happen to find
its way up your thigh,
would you object?
Or reach out for mine?

Can I close this space
between us?
And indulge in this carnal lust?
I want your skin to spark
in the wake of my touch.
I want you to feel nothing
but the heat of my love.

understand your effect

The bumps
living in my skin
only rise up for you
tempting sins
in their prompt response
to your unique blend
of forceful and soft
and fall they will not
even after
your tantalizing touch
has long stopped

I never had a chance

    Betrayed
        by the tremble in my touch
Seeing you this way
is almost too much.
   I fight
to regain my composure
as your shirt
    slowly slips
        from your shoulders
           (oh those shoulders...)
But you fire back
with a one-two attack
   warm breath
   tickling my neck
   as you quickly
   conquer my clasp
And here I thought
  I stood a chance

under these sheets

Flashes of lightning
  glowing neon purple white
     invade my room
and reverberate off the walls
    deafening
    my senses
commanding cracks
    sound waves arc
      relentless
     after-shocks
   racing down
my back
the electricity
surges through me
     rain pounding
       breath short
         en
          ing
skin
all but exposed
peeking
through
the thinnest of cotton
gladly
losing the fight
to hang on any longer

a knockout

No words.
I have no words.
Can't a girl
simply be impressed?

Between your ambitions
and that black dress
eloquence
never stood a chance.

on a July night

there's only one thing
I haven't stopped thinking about
all day,
one moment
I keep replaying
frame by frame
the slow motion
slide of a hand
followed by teeth
on tan skin
and remembering
how it feels to be let in
heads on chests
and the calming
of quickened breath
rediscovering
the quiet excitement
of crossing that line
for the first time

chapstick kisses

Peppermint tingles
the skin your lips visited
up, down, all around

don't stop

Sweat
and fingertips
    trailblazers
of the long way home
    charters of the wild
spread out
      across this skin

Anticipation
and
Fists
wrapped up in sheets
    torn from the mattress
      underneath

Destroyers
of order

Anchors
  for the storm
    you've unleashed

day dreaming

Oh, to slowly appreciate
every inch
and every curve
that your body has to offer.
To savor
every twitch
and every tremble
to even the faintest graze.
Wrapped in satin,
and high off the way you rise up.
Oh, to completely lose myself
drowning
in the sea of your pleasure.

can't hold it in

abandoning all inhibitions
    spurred on by a look
giving in to my affliction
    to my deepest animalistic level
    I have been shook
I can no longer stand here
and stall this urge

    Up against a wall

the passion inside starts to stir
and I will not rest
until your inhibitions too
    have come undone
Tell me now, if I'm too rough,
before my rational mind
completely shuts off
I will get so caught up,
drunkenly headstrong,
that my only thought will center on
quenching every thirst
you've ignored for too long

in silence

I didn't have to say a word
our eyes spoke the same language
All this biding
all the ones I've kept caged within
I feel like
  you've heard every last one
All that can't be boiled down
  to nouns or verbs
or even actions observed
  was found
  where our borders merged
In finding myself
I found you
and this loneliness cured

so why don't you

For once,
don't let conscience
intervene

For once,
let your body
take the lead

This attraction
cannot be
circumvened

Corporeal desires
will eventually
succeed

prowl on

A night beast
hankering for
a nice feast
spots its prey
stakes a course
and confidently
makes haste of feet.
In no time short
the unsuspecting
will be convinced
in the ravager's den
her night is best spent.

I can't get enough

Shadows have never
enticed me
as much as when they find refuge
in the fleshy sun-worn slopes
where strength protrudes.
It is the light
that has always drawn my attention,
but it has never engrossed me
such as it does
when it reflects off
the golden strands of your hair.
And I have known passion
but never of the variety
nor magnitude
of which you can conjure up
with the simple motion
of a single finger.

custom made love

my lips
    were born to seek out your spots
    those hot zones hidden in plain sight

these ears
    have been finely tuned
    to pick up on
    the subtle shifts
    in vibration
    of moanful cues

my touch
    evolved alongside
    the slightest quivers
    of sensitive skin

my eyes
    have grown glutton to
    the beginning corners
    of involuntary grins

I was built to love you
    made to fit you like a glove

Loss

now what

How can I dance
in this silence,
　when the beat is frozen
　　and the melody
　　　has faded away?
All this room to move
but the only two things
　twirling around now
are smoke
　　and memories of times of coy smiles
　　　and hands on the small of backs.

I never could dance,
I came built with too many kinks
between my shoulders and my feet
　they never could stay in sync.
Still,
I'd rather be a bumbling half
　than a waltzing whole
with nothing but ghosts of my past
　　to hold.

when nothing's left

The longing inside
fills every inch,
consumes every void
Screaming out for you

get up

Waking
to the sound of rain.
A Cleansing
to wash away
the pain.
Simply being
will lead to hurt
but the heavy drops
will wash away
the dirt.

for what?

How am I managing?
From where is the energy
for the next beat emerging?
Pushing on
and Pushing on
in this anaerobic love.
I do not know
how much longer
I can go on.

new breaths

Just give them all back
Every breath you stole from me
I'm suffocating

freed from exhaustion

I would have run
    circles and circles
      chasing after you
boundless circles for you
    with no starting
      and no finish line
circles that race to infinity
  never finding the end
    always chasing
      straining
after a light
    always on the move

    crazy

I would have gone crazy
    chasing after you

excused of the settle

She loves me
She loves me not
passing days
with the pluck of a petal

She loves me
She loves me not
all I can say
is I won't settle

She loves me
She loves me not
I refuse to concede
that its selfish
that you love me
with everything in you
or not at all

away it goes

day by day
I can feel the pieces of you
fly away
pieces that once made a whole
a whole that covered me,
consumed me
to my very soul
now its slowly
chipping away
like old paint
disappearing
with neglect and age

disappearing

The magic vanished
the day the tattered veil
was finally lifted.
There's nothing more
that can make me believe,
no sleight of hand,
no magic words,
not even the cleverest of misdirections.

I feel so foolish
for ever having fallen for any of it.
I'm sure you could see it:
the beguiled amazement
that twinkled in my eyes.
I know you ran
the day you realized
it died.

only to reappear

Being back here
I am confronted
by the ghosts of us.
From my mind
the serpentine shadows slip,
advantageously
through the cracks.
They flit about the room,
effervescing
through the people.
Dancing a dance of
stinging reenactment,
on which

I alone

am cursed to reflect,
of a time, oh so long ago.
I can blink
and they will flutter,
only too soon to be back.
They always find their way back.
I guess all I really have
are ghosts of you,
haunting me
in places you wouldn't
begin to imagine,
places that raise from the dead
times lost
and never to be had again.

then walk away again

How dare you give me that look
that leaves me floating on clouds.
All I've ever wanted is you,
but your actions speak so loud,
back-dropped by the silence
of no words to be found.
You have no place,
let alone time,
in your life for me.
So, forgive me, but
I can no longer go on
ignoring the sirens
blaring on my lawn.

you don't understand

Yours,
I am
and that knowledge kills me.

Forever Yours,
I am
and I could never fully
be anyone else's.

Hopelessly
and completely Yours,
I am
and the uncertainty fills me
not knowing
if you will ever claim me.

Yours,
can't you see that
I am?

how you stay

On my shirt
your scent
remains.
I breathe in
softly
slowly
fearful of
accelerating
the fade.
For no part of you
ever stays.

how I leave

You say you need space.
Knowing I can't save you kills.
There, is that enough?

what I lose

I miss your face.
I wonder if its changed.
Life is less alive
without you,
no matter the place.
I wonder if it shows on mine:
the incompleteness
I try to disguise.

how the music plays

The storm
raging outside my window
is the perfect soundtrack
for the struggle
tearing at my soul.
Those moments of calm
are full of deception.
Quicker than the close
of a heavy eye
and with a quaking vengeance
the discord will strike back
demanding recognition
while the grey skies
echo and amplify
the sorrow playing out inside.

what I'm trying to do

Falling every which way
floating and sinking
every other day

Beauty and heart so pure
with a confidence rare
but who's feelings can't be sure

Lucky, I know
to have, to hold
yet what do I have to show

But a weakened heart
a clown in a fool's parade
ever since the start

To give up, quit
just not my style
even through loss of wit

Occasions be known
of strength required
build it back stone by stone

Mind reign over heart
rose glasses aside
you must know when to part

this isn't helping

Please,
don't look at me like that,
you're making it really hard
to hold these feelings back.
I wish I didn't need a dam
for I would give you
all that I am.

Please,
don't reach for me
not when I'm this close
to breaking free.
I'll always mourn
what could have been
for you're not capable
of letting me in.

you still can't see

Go ahead–
    keep shutting me out
    and pushing me away
If ever comes the day
when you wake up
and realize
I'm the piece
that makes you whole
don't be surprised to find
you lost me long ago.

the fire

Fires don't always burn
without fuel and oxygen
      to ash they will turn

the hidden fissures

   this heart is nothing
but a volcano with your name
nothing but blood-red magma
trudging through these veins
burning vast tunnels
   and criss-crossing my soul
spewing ash,
   clouding my mind,
and oozing lava
that upon itself
    folds and folds
encapsulating
little moments in time
it may lay dormant
   every now and then
but where the eye can't see
love perpetually flows
   more thick than thin

the pins and needles

That prickly numb feeling
normally arisen
from circulation cut off,
overtakes my body
every time to you
turn my thoughts.

the delirium

I miss your signature blend
of sweet freshness
and spicy musk
a casual mingling
of the days' layers
of eau de parfums
waltzing across your skin

I can still make them out
if I focus hard enough

I miss that I will never
get high on them again

let's just end this

tell me
you don't love me
tell me
so maybe
just maybe
I can forget I ever did
I'll make believe
it was all
just a dream
and pretend
like
you never did hurt me
once and for all
just tell me

I'm trying

I'm trying really hard
to be strong
standing here
in front of you
but the logic
      the reasons
they just melt from me
dripping and puddling
      at my feet
a love that burns too hot
no strength can compete

and I'm failing

    Warming up the sheets
        was never hard with you
           but now I'm left
              to brave the cold
          starkly alone
            trying to remember
              the heat
                  this bed used to know

I'm all turned around

A hope so toxic
and built up thick.
This noxious gas
clouds the exit
and knocks me on my ass.
Immobilizing and
delirium rich.

   Now which way is which?

Why can't I stop
inhaling so quick
this stagnant air
that's making me sick?

I can't break free

  Every time I think
I have this whole
living-without-you thing down
  you show your face
and my whole course
is turned around
  Everything I've built up
comes crashing to the ground
In smooth waters
I was swimming
  but here you come
with your careless waves
and once again
in you I am drowned

My Lady Kryptonite

My Lady Kryptonite,
with ache
my heart
is perpetually dyed.
Shattered.
With no end in sight
to my anguish and torment.
All my power
has been spent.
Your cold
sheds me of my leaves
and chokes out all hope
of a Spring.
Inside
I wither and writhe.
Living while I slowly die.
Kiss me once more,
my Lady Kryptonite.

you make it look so easy

Once again
you have flown away
    my bird of many feathers.
And there is
  but the slightest
    of comfort
      in knowing
I couldn't have loved you
any better

but I see through it

That's not gonna work.
I've bitten and been hooked
by far less than that before,
but this time...
    this time its gonna take much more.
I've been conditioned
not to take things at face value,
to constantly question
what to believe as true.
I've been hardened
and I hate it,
but without that extra strength
I never would have made it.

I can't give enough

My love
    ...my love,
I know these words
are not enough,
but you see
deep run the cuts,
jagged, raw and rough.
Eventually
the stitches will hold
and gone will be the cold.
But when?
I cannot know.
It's unfair,
this blind patience
of you I ask
but you deserve more
than a heart
crippled
and bound by a cast.

seen too much

The shadows play tricks on me
convincing me of things
that aren't to be believed.
Excitement
and disappointment
live on opposing sides
of a bewildered blink.
Forced to do a double-take
only to be fooled again by instinct.

torn and undone

I must have lost you
with the setting of the sun,
a goodbye so beautiful
how could I have known
that in the creep of night
we would be undone.

I must have lost you
with the setting of the sun,
for when I was torn asunder
unceremoniously
from the warm cocoon of my slumber
all around me hung
a suffocating cacophony of despair
and chilling curtains of glum.

I must have lost you
with the setting of the sun,
the cold has really settled in now
not even your shadow hung around
such a painful way to tell me
we're done.

transparent

Fight it?
I guess I could try,
but what's the use
when you're the reason
to my why.

Hide it?
If only I could,
but my eyes
they give it away
upon you they fall
and they stay.

Encourage it?
I can't. I won't.
Not while you fight and hide.
Not while you deny
all that's inside.

I'm still standing

my emotional leech
you're slowly sucking
the life
the strength
out of me
but
for you I stand tall
even as the buttresses
fail to support
my wobbly walls

after everything

Laying sprawled
on hot asphalt.
Drifting out
but brought back in
by flashing lights
overhead.
Just another victim
of a reckless love's
hit and run.

it lives on

If you told me tomorrow
that the love is gone
and we will never be
I would lie to myself
    saying it's all meant to be
    that one day my true love
    will come around.
I would lie
until it felt real,
mind resting sound
with the lies believed.
    But my heart
she is tenacious
and not so easily deceived.
    From deep down
a small reminder would creep
    upon merely
    the breathing of your name
    upon even
    the slightest trace of your face
of the love she still keeps.

in shadows

It is gone,
the spark inside me
that gave rise
to wonder and brilliance
of the likes
I had never seen before
or since.

It is gone,
but the burned shadow remains
mocking me
and all I have lost.

emerging anew

you didn't want me
and that's okay
the narcissist within me
has finally let me see
that that's okay

but truthfully
I'm fucking great
and you're crazy

but it's okay
really
because I'm no longer
burning my love
for a never-gonna-come
someday

my gift to you

Love, Lust and Loss
You know you're never really gone
In those words
until the sun no longer dawns
you will live on
My proudest achievement
ironically born
from my greatest loss
and hardest bereavement
In ink scarred paper
dripping with the blood of first love
I found a way to ease the hurt
and remember why it is
I loved you so much
for better or for worse

about the author

A Texas native and Oklahoma transplant, B. Grissom enjoys creating, no matter the medium. She is happiest when basking in the sun, surrounded by the laughter of friends. She is also acutely aware of her inability to refrain from being a complete and total dork, but wears the title like a badge of honor.

Follow on Instagram @beezerb

Made in the USA
Coppell, TX
30 October 2021